Business Gold:
Build Awareness, Authority, and Advantage with LinkedIn Company Pages

By

Michelle J Raymond   *Lynnaire Johnston*

Imprint Page

First published in 2021 by Michelle J Raymond and Lynnaire Johnston.

A catalogue entry for this book is available from the National Library of New Zealand.

Paperback: ISBN 978-0-473-60510-0

Kindle: ISBN 978-0-473-60512-4

Epub: ISBN 978-0-473-60511-7

The paper this book is printed on is certified as environmentally friendly.

Disclaimer

Contents

Foreword

That you are reading **Business Gold** is a testament to the power of LinkedIn on a global scale to bring about opportunities. It has come about, as many things do, via a circuitous route.

LinkedIn Pages Specialist Michelle J Raymond, based in Australia, met Vietek Ladislaav through commenting on mutual connections' posts. She was subsequently invited as a guest on his podcast *LinkedIn Smart* to talk about her experience and knowledge of LinkedIn Pages. (https://redcircle.com/shows/linkedin-smart)

LinkedIn expert and author Lynnaire Johnston, based in New Zealand, heard the episode and was impressed with Michelle's eloquence on the subject. She too believed that company Pages were the future of LinkedIn and reached out to Michelle.

A Zoom call was set up, and in that way LinkedIn makes you feel like you already know someone before you 'meet' them, the synergy between them was apparent. In under 15 minutes, Lynnaire suggested she and Michelle collaborate on a book about LinkedIn Pages with Michelle, the subject matter expert and Lynnaire, the writer.

Michelle was excited as Lynnaire had already written a successful book, *Link·Ability, 4 powerful strategies to maximise your LinkedIn success*. Likewise, Lynnaire was thrilled that her plan to write a book about company Pages now had Michelle's expertise behind it.

Together they have utilised the best of each other's skills to create the world's first book focussing on LinkedIn Pages to help others learn from their experience and knowledge.

Their message to you: Never underestimate what can be achieved using LinkedIn.

About the Authors

Michelle J Raymond

Michelle J Raymond is the Chief LinkedIn Strategist at her company Good Trading Co and a founding member of the LinkedIn Small Business Advisory Council for LinkedIn Pages. She's an innovator and thought leader who helps purpose-driven businesses thrive by creating sustainable strategies for growth, using social selling techniques on LinkedIn.

Michelle specialises in helping small to medium business owners make a real impact in business. She takes a hands-on approach, integrating her services into existing teams and working closely with companies on strategy execution and practical implementation of successful LinkedIn marketing campaigns.

Michelle thrives on sharing the stories of unique businesses to increase their visibility and harness the power of their unique selling point.

Michelle trains clients to attract new opportunities to increase revenue, build a solid reputation and position their brand for success.

As a leading global authority on LinkedIn Pages, her passion is to change the world by doing good business with good people.

Reach Michelle at michelle@goodtradingco.com.au or https://www.linkedin.com/in/michelle-raymond-goodtradingco/

Lynnaire Johnston

Lynnaire Johnston is an internationally recognised LinkedIn expert and author of *Link·Ability, 4 powerful strategies to maximise your LinkedIn success.*

As a LinkedIn strategist and practitioner, she helps business professionals use LinkedIn to achieve their business goals. Whether they are looking to be known as the expert in their field, drive customers and leads, or meet and network with those at the highest echelons of their industry – LinkedIn can help them do that, and Lynnaire advises them how.

She also runs a LinkedIn marketing programme, a done-for-you service of publishing and network building for busy business professionals.

Ranked among the Top 20 LinkedIn experts Asia Pacific by the Social Media Marketing Institute (Australia), Lynnaire has created the world's first LinkedIn members site for those who are serious about LinkedIn. Find out more at
https://www.wordwizard.co.nz/membership/

Her varied career has encompassed radio, publishing, local government and not-for-profit. Based in New Zealand, Lynnaire runs the communications company Word Wizard.

As an internationally recognised LinkedIn expert, her passion is to contribute to the success of others by simplifying LinkedIn and delivering solutions that help them make sense of the platform.

Reach Lynnaire at lynnaire@wordwizard.co.nz or https://www.linkedin.com/in/lynnairejohnston/

Part 1 — Awareness

Chapter 1
Why Businesses Need a LinkedIn Company Page

LinkedIn began life as a recruitment site. It was where people looking for work and those searching for potential workers went to find them. The job-seekers uploaded their CVs or resumés and hoped employers and recruiters would find them.

The second iteration of LinkedIn began when it became possible to publish on the platform, which encouraged business professionals of all types to start building their personal brands and networks. This allowed individuals to develop a reputation as a thought leader in their field and become known as an expert in their respective industry.

Business owners, solopreneurs, entrepreneurs, freelancers, consultants and other professionals began to see the potential of LinkedIn to help them reach their target audiences through content and outreach.

Voted the Most Trusted Digital Platform (Business Insider 2020 report) four years in a row, LinkedIn continues to go from strength to strength, setting records for the number of users and revenue milestones.

Owners of businesses of all sizes can make good use of the way LinkedIn has been reinvigorated under new CEO Ryan Roslansky and Microsoft's ownership.

LinkedIn's motto is 'Do Business Where Business is Done'. By making LinkedIn Company Pages (officially known as Pages) more functional and useful, LinkedIn encourages businesses to use them as part of their B2B marketing strategy.

While some growth remains in the recruitment side of the business, and increasing member numbers mean more sales of paid accounts such as Premium and Sales Navigator, that growth is limited.

It is essential to understand that LinkedIn currently generates a significant portion of revenue through paid advertising. However, you are not able to run a paid ad campaign without first setting up a Page.

Both authors acknowledge that, historically, Pages' functionality was clunky at best and still has a way to go. LinkedIn has however been consistently making changes to Pages, adding new sections, functions, analytics and features during 2020/21.

These changes are designed to make Pages more eye-catching, improve ease of use, and bring employees or staff together in one centralised place. (There is a full explanation of the features of Pages in chapter 2).

At present, there is no direct cost to set up a Page, thus making them attractive to businesses of all sizes. The organic reach for Pages is a mostly level playing field for businesses of all sizes. LinkedIn has not become as saturated as some other platforms where companies have to 'pay to play'. Solid organic reach can be built over time, and in this book, we explain how.

Business professionals who use LinkedIn as part of their marketing strategy do so to build credibility, increase visibility and become the go-to person in their industry. But these goals are not confined to individuals. Companies, too, need to develop or expand their presence, brand awareness and authority. They need to be seen as professional, competent and trustworthy. LinkedIn is an ideal platform to help them achieve this.

Companies using LinkedIn for their marketing have a great opportunity to harness the networks of their employees. For instance, if an organisation has 10 staff, all of whom have 1,000 connections, that's a potential audience of more than 10,000 for Page posts, in addition to the Page's followers. And on LinkedIn, getting in front of sufficient numbers of the right people is the key to being seen. By encouraging your team to advocate for your company through LinkedIn, both you and they win. There's more about how to do this in chapter 5, How to Publish on LinkedIn Pages.

Another benefit of Pages in terms of employees, is that your company logo will appear on their personal Profile if they add the company to their Experience section – a great advertisement for you and one that continues to occur well after they have left your organisation. This helps you attract high-calibre candidates for your vacancies, especially if your Page content meets their expectations around shared values. Your Page, in effect, has two audiences – potential customers or clients and potential employees.

For small businesses, solopreneurs, coaches and consultants, Pages can be a low-cost alternative to a website, albeit a simple one. It is an easy way to achieve visibility without a significant investment in website design and development.

An additional bonus is that LinkedIn Pages often show up on page one of Google search results for company names. It also gives you free organic reach, making it easier for potential customers to find you. Achieving good traffic levels to your website can be hard work, so a Page makes a great alternative.

Websites are usually static, and changing them can take time, whereas Pages allow business owners to update content and reach potential buyers more easily. In addition, through your posts, events, and other activities, they can get a good feel for your organisation, what it stands for, how it works, and how your solutions will help them.

If your company is relatively new, you may not yet have gained significant brand awareness. A Page can solve this. By setting it up well, inviting connections to follow your Page and consistently publishing high-quality content, your brand will gain visibility and recognition.

We, the authors, are watching the development of Pages closely. We know that they are currently often dismissed as unimportant, useless and not worth spending time on. While acknowledging this may have been true in the past, the impact of COVID-19 on business globally saw their importance both change and elevate.

By the time you read this, we expect Pages to have become **_Business Gold_** for companies actively using the platform to build brand awareness, educate potential clients, and create a strong following of motivated and engaged clients and staff.

Of course, as was the case with Facebook in 2017, there will likely come a time when posts from Pages need to be boosted or paid for to achieve substantial organic reach. But, right now, all businesses, no matter what their size or employee strength, can use Pages to make an impact on LinkedIn. And in this book, we show you how.

Gold Nuggets

Why you should be paying attention to Pages:

- They're currently free.

- Setting up a basic Page is very easy, with multiple opportunities to make it impactful.

- If you want to run a paid campaign on LinkedIn, you'll need a LinkedIn Page. Preferably one with a good following.

- It's an excellent way to promote more content to your target audience.

- With 100 invite credits per month available, you can quickly grow your following.

- Linking your personal Profile to your company by updating your work experience displays your logo in the Experience section and at the top of employees' Profiles.

- You can post different content from your Profile and your Page, giving you two separate streams of content.

- You can set up sub-Pages, known as Showcase Pages and Product Pages, which are ideal for creating an audience for a specific product or service, brand or location with a defined audience.

- Posting from Pages can attract a significant number of organic impressions.

- Multiple Page Admins can be added to help manage the Page.

- When your team members get behind your Page, your reach expands exponentially.

- The analytics from your Page are comprehensive and don't require a paid account or third-party application to review.

- You can drive traffic to your landing page or website from your Page.

- Your Page can help you attract further business opportunities.

- You can hold events from your Page to build brand awareness and generate leads.

Chapter 2
What's On a LinkedIn Page

LinkedIn Pages offer a raft of features that are not available on personal Profiles. Conversely, Profiles have features not available on Pages. But given that Pages and Profiles have different roles, this is no surprise. And certainly, Pages offer advantages that Profiles do not have.

This chapter is an overview of what you'll find on Pages which we discuss in more detail in subsequent chapters. The more you understand the puzzle pieces, the more you can take full advantage of and get Pages working for you.

It is easy to skip over details during the setup stage. Often there are good intentions to come back around and complete missing information, but somehow, we never quite get to it. This will impact the reach of your Page.

If your Page has already been set up, we recommend you go back over and check the setup is in line with current best practices and that the Page is 100% completed.

Cover image

The first thing visitors to the Page will see is the cover image (sometimes referred to as a banner). It's where you can make a strong, positive impression in the blink of an eye. It's what will make a visitor stop to find out more, or move on to another Page and never read a word of yours.

The size of the LinkedIn Page cover image differs from personal Profiles and is 1128 x 191 pixels. Allow space on the left third of the cover image for your logo to display.

If you do not upload your cover image, this is displayed by default:

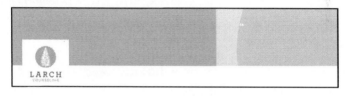

You can see that it does nothing to enhance your company's reputation. Instead, it shows that you do not value your Page sufficiently to make an effort to create and upload one. LinkedIn cover images are easily created in Canva, which can be accessed for free. A simple abstract or a geographical image is better than none at all.

Here is an example of a LinkedIn cover image from co-author Lynnaire Johnston's Page.

Logo

The small square at the bottom left of the cover image section contains the company's logo.

Below is an example of co-author Michelle J Raymond's Page – Good Trading Co.

An additional benefit of updating the Page logo is that it will display correctly in the Experience section on the personal Profile of any team member who has updated their experience and selected the matching Page.

If the employee believes they have updated their Profile and still the logo is missing, this could be a misnamed company name, or the Page may have been created after the Experience section was updated.

Once the Experience section matches the correct Page, the team member automatically becomes a Page follower. This will also ensure they can potentially be notified of new content that has been posted.

For current employees, the logo also displays at the top right of their Profile, making it advantageous from a company branding perspective for team members to indicate this.

If you do not upload an image to the logo section, visitors will see a default image supplied by LinkedIn. However, the default image creates a lack of trust, so it's best to get this updated.

Page logos must be 300 x 300 pixels. This is tricky for companies with logos that are longer than they are wide, as they do not display well in this square format.

With the introduction of Dark Mode, company logo images are displayed on both light and dark backgrounds. If your logo is transparent, it will be shown on a white background which may impact how it looks. We recommend testing your logo to make sure it displays correctly on both light and dark backgrounds.

Tagline

The tagline for your organisation is the equivalent of a Profile headline. It sits under your company name in the top section of the Page and is a short 120 characters.

This would most likely be the punchy catchphrase the company uses, but it can also be used as a short description of the products or services provided.

Overview

The overview is a 2,000-character (around 250 words) description of your business. It displays under the title About on the Home tab and under Overview on the About tab.

This section should include keywords and phrases to enhance the chance of your Page appearing in organic search results.

Company details

The information required here is relatively straightforward and includes:

- Company website address
- Industry your company operates in
- Company size
- Company type
- Phone number
- Year founded
- Specialties (up to 20) – these are important to assist with organic search results
- Languages
- Locations
- Workplace Module – optional. Attract top candidates by highlighting your workplace benefits and policies. Select from Onsite, Hybrid, or Remote for your workplace.
- Hashtags – currently three hashtags that the Page follows, which will become more important in the future.

Call to action buttons

When someone visits your Page for the first time, they are greeted by a big blue button sitting at the top in the introductory section. This indicates the action you would like them to take. Options are Follow (the Page), Visit website, Contact us, Learn more, Register and Sign up.

Be strategic with your choice and align the selection with your business goals. Always go back and check that existing links are working, and are still the best option for your business.

For example, if you select the Contact Us button, make sure that the link takes users directly to your Contact page on your website and not the generic Home page. If your goal is to grow your mailing list, 'Sign up' would be a much better option.

The fewer clicks people have to make, the less chance you have of losing them.

It is important to note that Pages have no option for direct messaging with Page followers at the time of writing. This is currently managed through the Call-to-Action (CTA) button.

Admin tools

The functions available to an admin sit at the top right corner of the Page. They include Invite connections, Sponsor an update, Post a job, Create an event, Create a Showcase Page, Settings (which allow you to manage admins and deactivate the Page) and other administrative functions such as help, feedback, and Terms and Conditions.

Page admin view – navigation bar

At the top of each Page are the navigation buttons – All Pages (Home/My Company), Products, Content, Analytics, and Activity. These sit above the banner and are viewable by Page admins.

Home – this is the main tab that Page admins use and covers a wide range of features such as:

- Analytics for the last 30 days includes unique visitors, new followers, post impressions, and custom button clicks. Each of these displays more detail when clicked.

- Start a Post

- Manage Events

- Manage Hashtags

- Invite Connections

- Showcase Pages and other Affiliated Pages

- Customised Feeds.

My company – is an employee-only experience on the navigation bar of the introduction section, but is only visible when there are more than ten associated employees.

Content – this displays trending articles, employee milestones, and company news.

Recommend to employees – this is a trusted employee-only space that makes it easy for large companies to have employees connect, celebrate employee milestones, build employee advocacy and interact with co-workers. It displays trending co-worker content (posts), allows team members to see their co-workers and for them to connect with suggested new ones.

LinkedIn Pages analytics

Tracking Page performance within LinkedIn without the need for a third-party app, is one of the advantages of LinkedIn Pages. However, the analytics available on mobile and desktop is slightly different. Therefore, in most cases, it is better to use this feature on the desktop version.

Detailed reports can be reviewed over customised periods. There is also an opportunity to download an .xls file for monitoring and reporting.

Visitors – these analytics are beneficial to see if your Page is attracting the right audience. This can be displayed by job function, location, seniority, industry, or company size.

Updates – the analytics shown here allow Page admins a view of how the content is performing for both organic and paid content. Monitor this over time and review what content is performing best with your Page followers. Some of the analytics here are clicks, views, impressions, CTR, reactions, comments, shares etc.

Followers – this is where you can find all your Page followers and visit their Profiles with a view to connecting with them.

Competitors – the most recent addition to analytics allows you to select up to nine other Pages you would like to compare your Page against. The comparison is limited to just followers and engagements but will be a time saver for those previously reporting manually.

Employee Advocacy – having employees share content to their personal networks is important, and these analytics allow you to monitor the success of internal initiatives. These analytics are based on employees posting the 'recommended content' from Page admins.

Activity – monitoring Page activity allows admins to filter by requests, comments, mentions, posts, shares, and reactions. These are displayed in a newsfeed style with a Post highlights section to the right, and thumbnails of the Most commented and Most reacted posts of the last 30 days. Activity is divided into Updates (posts) and Events.

Member View – Navigation Bar

Page visitors will see these navigation buttons at the bottom of the Page's introduction section: Home, About, Posts, Jobs, People, Insights and Events. Click on each of these to go to that section of the Page:

- Home – this shows the Page's About section and posts
- About – this shows the Overview and company location
- Posts – this shows all the posts published on the Page.

Jobs – this allows you to attract qualified applicants by posting and showcasing jobs on your Page.

People – this shows some details about the company's employees and includes a 'People you may know' section.

Insights – are only displayed when there are 30 or more complete member Profiles from the company the

Page belongs to. The view which is available to Premium subscription members allows more research to be done on the company.

Events – this shows upcoming and previous events.

Video Tab – this shows any videos and LinkedIn lives the Page has published.

From all this, you can see that Pages provide a great deal more information than is available from personal Profiles. This lends further credence to our assertion that Pages are where the next generation of activity on LinkedIn will come from. Plus, by the time you read this book, additional features are likely to have been added.

Gold Nuggets

- Pages contain many features not available on personal Profiles.

- Completing all sections of a Page improves visibility and reach.

- Adding an eye-catching cover image engenders trust with visitors.

- Including keywords in the Overview improves organic search results.

- Choose your CTA button wisely and link to a specific page on your website for best results.

- LinkedIn says Pages with complete information receive 30% more weekly views.

Chapter 3
How LinkedIn Pages Differ from Profiles

On LinkedIn, Pages and Profiles are entirely different beasts. They differ in their purpose, features, publishing and use.

Purpose

By definition, Pages are by and about a company; Profiles are by and about an individual.

A Page is set up by a LinkedIn member who has a Profile. By default, they become the Page admin. In other words, a company cannot set up a Page without it being associated with a Profile.

Page admins run and control the Page and upload content. Anyone can be made a Page admin, and there are several levels of admin that serve different purposes. We discuss these in chapter 4.

On Profiles, those who are in the person's network are called either Connections or Followers; Pages only have Followers. Profile holders are limited to sending approximately 100 connections per week; Pages are given 100 invites per month. If an invite to a Page is accepted, an invite credit is returned, which can be used to invite another person.

Invite credits can only be used by Page admins and can only be sent to first degree connections. This is an excellent reason to have more than one Page admin per Page. However, the monthly invite maximum is not per admin; it is per Page. So more admins, unfortunately, doesn't mean more invites are available. It does, however, allow you to share the workload.

Features

Profiles are highly visual and offer multiple opportunities to showcase skills, abilities, experience, media, education, accomplishments, recommendations, etc. The main Page is limited in scope but is supported by more options on linked Showcase Pages and Product Pages. Though at the speed at which Pages are changing, this may not remain true.

At present, the information able to be displayed on a Page is limited to:

- A 2,000-character About or Overview section
- Website URL
- Location
- Industry
- Company size and type
- Phone number
- Year when founded
- Up to 20 specialties.

None of this is visual, except the location map. People cannot endorse a company on a Page, and neither can it showcase its social responsibility activities or the organisations it supports.

On a Page, there is no Featured section or the ability to add media. Neither can Page followers leave recommendations. Fortunately, these are all addressed by Product Pages, which allow the addition of media, recommendations, and customers using your product. See more about Product Pages in chapter 8.

Where Pages and Profiles dovetail is through the Page logo. This appears on the Profile of a person who has in their Experience section, that they do or did work for the company. One of the downsides of Pages is that anyone can claim to work for an organisation and display the company logo on their Profile. A Page admin cannot remove an inaccurate employee directly but must reach out to LinkedIn [https://bit.ly/3FDkEiw] for help.

Publishing

While Pages and Profiles appear to be miles apart in terms of looks, they are more similar when it comes to publishing or posting. LinkedIn has begun offering more publishing formats for Pages, and now all those available on Profiles (text, image and document posts, videos, polls and articles) are available on Pages.

Page followers can now search posts by format through the menu on the Posts tab (above). Posts can be engaged with in the same way as they are on Profiles through reactions, comments and shares.

One type of engagement that is not commonly seen is Pages commenting on posts. To date, the functionality does not make this simple unless the Page is tagged (@mentioned) or the post contains one of the three hashtags the company has nominated (see chapter 2). Unfortunately, if the Page does comment, there is no notification of a response, which could damage the company's reputation if a reply goes unanswered. This is a feature the authors hope will be added in upcoming releases.

Use of Pages

Another difference between Pages and Profiles is that paid advertising is only possible with a Page. However, the authors believe that Pages provide plenty of opportunities for organic reach, and these should be thoroughly explored before considering a paid media strategy. LinkedIn advertising is expensive relative to other social media platforms and is often out of reach for small businesses. If you have the budget, understand your target audience and know the content that works for your audience, then advertising may be worth exploring.

Pages become more attractive for larger companies and those with multiple audiences using Showcase, Product and Affiliate Pages. These are covered in chapter 8.

How much time should you spend on your Page?

Social media, in general, can quickly drain a lot of time and focus if you don't have clear goals and a strategy in place to meet them.

Your Page is the same. Start with your goals and work backwards. These may be building brand awareness, gaining visibility, lead generation or something else entirely. Whatever your goals, they should be aligned with the company's overall business strategy.

Once you know your goals, look at the available time to create content and manage the online community. It is a task that requires consistency to be effective, so it is better to overestimate than underestimate this.

As you build your processes, tasks will become easier and take less time. So don't be tempted to give up too quickly.

Develop a checklist of tasks that need regular attention and delegate them to the appropriate person or people. Track their completion and make changes if those such as inviting connections to follow the Page are not accomplished in a timely fashion.

If you find that it is impossible to get the workload completed after a trial period of three months, reach out to the authors and discuss outsourcing.

Gold Nuggets

- Pages and Profiles work differently in terms of their purposes, features, publishing and use.

- Many of the features of Profiles are not available on Pages, but this is changing.

- The publishing formats available on Pages and Profiles are now the same.

- Knowing what you want your Page to achieve will help with its management and content creation.

Part 2 — Authority

Chapter 4
How to Set up a LinkedIn Page for Your Business

When you begin to set up your Page, you'll notice it is entirely different to a personal Profile.

Creating your Page is not difficult and doesn't take a lot of time. A basic setup will take around 30-60 minutes. A Page should be refined over time as your business changes to meet different demands.

Step 1 – Create the Page

- Log into your personal LinkedIn account on a desktop computer as Pages cannot be created on a mobile device.

- Click on the Work waffle in the top right-hand corner of the main menu.

- From the drop-down menu, select Create a Company Page + at the bottom (see image).

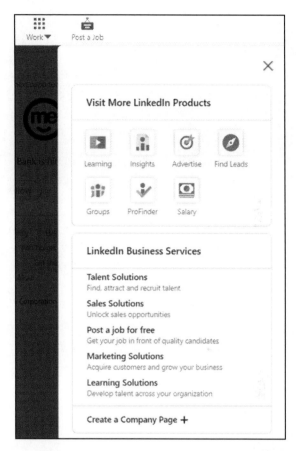

Step 2 – Select the type of business appropriate for you.

- Click on either the Small business or Medium to large business icon. (Do not choose Showcase page or Educational institution.)

Step 3 – Complete your Page identity

- Complete your business name. LinkedIn will automatically create a public URL. If your business name is ambiguous, consider adding what you do to the end of the company name. If there are other companies with the same name, find a new way to write it, such as adding Limited or Pty, or your location (e.g. Aus).

- Complete the URL of your company website.

---

* indicates required

Page identity

Name*

[   ]

LinkedIn public URL* ❓

linkedin.com/company/ [   ]

Website

[Begin with http:// or https:// or www.   ]

This is a link to your external website.

Step 4 – Complete the company details section

- Select industry, company size and company type from the drop-down lists.

  (If your industry is not listed, you need to choose the next closest option.)

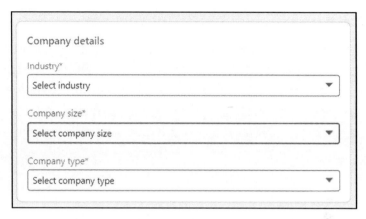

- Specialties should be added and take full advantage of a maximum of 20. Utilise keywords that will assist with your Page showing in search results.

Step 5 – Complete the Profile details

- Click choose file and upload your logo. The recommended dimensions are square 300 x 300 pixels. If your logo does not display well, you may need to use Squoosh [https://squoosh.app/] or Canva [https://www.canva.com/] to resize it or get a different design entirely.

- Write a powerful 120-character tagline that communicates your brand promise in a clear, concise and memorable way. Try a few different taglines to see which is best. Unlike headlines on Profiles, taglines do not accompany the logo when used elsewhere on the platform, such as in comments.

- When a Page comments, the logo and number of followers are displayed, although this is not ideal if your Page does not have a reasonable number of followers.

- Check the verification box, then click Create Page.

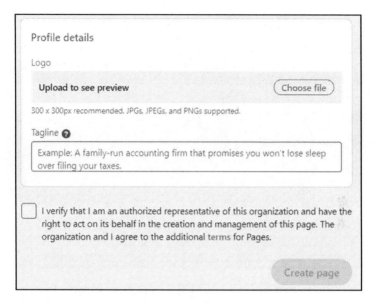

Step 6 – Add a Cover image

- Click on the pencil in the top right-hand corner and upload an image that is 1128 x 191 pixels. It is best to avoid putting important design features in the first third (from the left) of the cover image as the Page logo will hide this. Even if there is no logo, the box it sits in, is always visible.

- When creating your cover image, make the words as large as possible to ensure they can be easily seen when viewed on the mobile app.

- Canva has free templates you can use to create your image. Alternatively, getting this cover image designed by a professional is a worthwhile investment.

- Your cover image should convey what your company does, who the target market is and how you help them. The image and words achieve this together, so it is worth putting time into getting it right.

Step 7 – Build your Page

- Complete the various action cards shown.

- Click Add to open and complete each section, including your location.

- It is crucial to complete each section, but it is unnecessary to post if you're not ready.

Step 8 – Choose a Custom button to display

- In the Overview section, select one of the following custom button names from the drop-down box – Contact Us, Learn More, Register, Sign Up, Visit Website.

- Add your website URL but make it targeted, so that potential clients are directed to a specific and the most direct page on your website. Here are two examples:

Learn More redirecting to
https://www.wordwizard.co.nz/membership/

Contact Us button redirecting to
https://goodtradingco.com.au/contact-us/

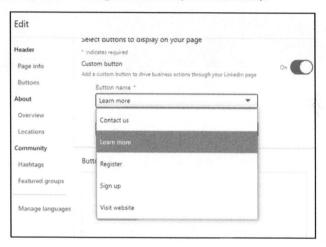

Step 9 – Provide Details to display

- Description – write a clear and concise explanation of the services or products you offer up to 2,000-characters long.

- Format it to be easy to read, ideally with two sentences per paragraph and spaces between paragraphs. As a dense block of text can be off-putting and hard to read, we recommend you break up the text using emojis.

The key information the About description needs to cover is:

- Your business product or services

- Your target market

- How you deliver – online store, 1-2-1 coaching sessions etc

- What clients or customers get out of it – the benefits or results

- The company's contact details, website URL and socials should be listed to make it easy for customers and clients to find you and get in touch with you.

Overview

Is your business missing out on growth opportunities because you are invisible on the world's No1 platform for B2B buyers?

Top 5 Reasons Your Business needs a Company Page
- If your buyers are professionals or businesses, there are 774M+ users + 58M companies on LinkedIn (and growing).
- Company brand awareness – use this in synergy with your employee personal brands for greater results for both.
- Build company thought leadership using content and Events with Page followers.
- Engage your employees. Employee advocacy is a powerful tool.
- Attract top talent.

We Help LinkedIn Page Administrators with -
- Company Page Setup
- Company Page Audits and Strategy
- 1-1 Consulting
- Page Administrators Training – learn how to get the most out of your Page
- Company Page Management – if you don't have resources internally then it's time to outsource

We work with -
Solopreneurs, Consultants, Small-Medium Business Owners, Digital Agencies, Marketing teams, Social Media Managers and Page Administrators.

Especially enjoy training women 50+ consultants who are subject matter experts but doubt themselves when it comes to social media. We want you to have confidence and shine!

About Good Trading Co.
Owned and operated by global LinkedIn Pages expert and trainer Michelle J Raymond. Michelle is a member of the LinkedIn Pages Small Business Advisory Council and tests new features in conjunction with the LinkedIn Pages Product team.

Using her 15+ years of sales experience Michelle loves to work with clients to-
- Help them identify their unique selling points
- Become laser focussed on their ideal customer
- Create a content strategy that talks to these strengths to build brand awareness and generate leads.

Would love to hear from you - michelle@goodtradingco.com.au

Step 10 – Choose your company locations

- Click on + Add a location.

You may enter multiple locations or none if you do not have a public office.

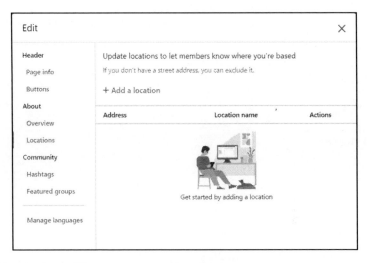

Edit　　　　　　　　　　　　　　　　　　　　　　×

Header　　　Update locations to let members know where you're based

　Page info　　If you don't have a street address, you can exclude it.

　Buttons　　+ Add a location

About

　　　　　　　Address　　　　　Location name　　　　　Actions

　Overview

　Locations

Community

　Hashtags

　Featured groups

　　　　　　　　　　Get started by adding a location

　Manage languages

Step 11 – Choose your hashtags

- Click on + Add a Hashtag

- Choose up to three hashtags to associate with your Page. The importance of this selection has recently become more critical. The hashtags you choose appear in a news feed on the Home Page. From here, the Page can comment on posts that use the followed hashtags.

The hashtag selected for your Page is something that you will need to trial for quality of content. Our recommendation is to choose some mega/general hashtags as well as a smaller niche. Then, it can be easily changed based on the quality of your feed. This will build your business credibility and authority.

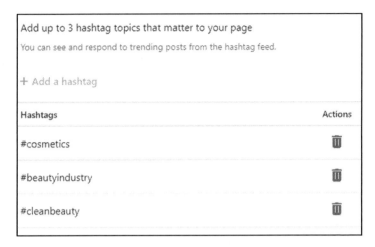

Step 12 – Add LinkedIn groups

- If your company also has a group set-up, add this information here. Otherwise, skip this.

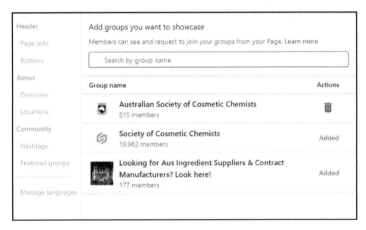

Step 13 – Add languages

- Click + Add a language if you operate a bi- or multi-lingual business.

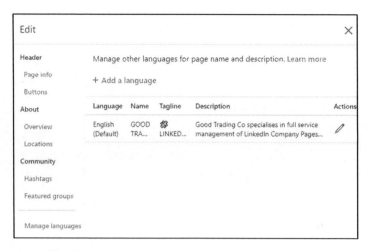

Page admins

Once you have created the Page, you need to decide who will have what level of access. By default, the person who sets up the Page is the owner of the Page. Although this is where the Page's control resides, it is essential never to lose this through an employee leaving or other factors beyond your control.

It is now possible to add admins and assign various roles to people who aren't first degree connections, which had been a considerable limitation.

You can add or remove admins from the Admin tools button on the top right of your Page.

From the Settings menu, click Manage admins.

As LinkedIn Help says, there are several admin levels:

- Super admin – this gives access to every Page admin function available, including adding and removing any admin on the Page, editing Page information, and deactivating the Page. Your main landing Page is the Super admin view.

39

- Content admin – this gives permission to create and manage page content, including updates (and boosting updates), Events, and Jobs. The main landing Page for this level is Content admin view.

- Curator – this gives permission to view Content suggestions, create recommended content, and view and export Page analytics.

- Analyst – this gives permission to monitor the Page's analytics to help drive goals. Analysts have limited access to the Page via 3rd party tools. Their only access is to the Analytics tab of a Page.

In addition to internal admins, there are also paid media admin options:

- Sponsored Content Poster – this gives permission to create Sponsored content ads on behalf of an organisation through your LinkedIn Ads account. This role doesn't grant access to boosting organic updates directly on a Page (see content admin information above).

- Lead Gen Forms Manager – this gives permission to download leads received from the Page. This is tied to Lead generation forms that are created in ads accounts through Campaign Manager.

- Pipeline Builder – this gives permission to create and edit Pipeline Builder landing Pages that are associated with your Page.

Page Creation Mistakes to Avoid

1. Incomplete Information

One of the primary mistakes people make is not ensuring that the information on their Page is complete. Leaving gaps reflects poorly on your company. It gives the viewer the impression that you are a company that doesn't pay attention to detail and cuts corners. This does not assist in building trust or credibility.

2. Not notifying employees

Once a Page has been created, make sure you notify employees. Request that they update their Profile Experience, which automatically makes them followers of the Page and displays the company logo on their Profile.

Creating this link from their Profile to the Page allows them to receive notifications when you produce content.

3. Having only one Page admin

Too often, Pages are set up with access for only one company employee. This is fraught with danger. If that employee leaves on bad terms, it will be challenging to regain control of the Page.

Having multiple admins is the best practice and will always ensure at least one person can access and manage it.

Gold Nuggets

- Your cover image is excellent free advertising space and an opportunity for you to make it clear what you do. It is prime real estate and should be treated as such.

- Add your best contact details to make it easy for prospective clients to contact you. It can never be in too many places because people are notoriously lazy at looking for them.

- Your tagline should be completed in line with your mission statement or company slogan.

- Make sure your Page reflects your company personality. While LinkedIn is a professional platform, it doesn't need to be boring, and your Page will stand out if it is different or quirky.

Chapter 5
How to Publish on LinkedIn Pages

One of the most important reasons to put time and effort into LinkedIn Pages is posting content from them. This has multiple benefits, namely building visibility on the platform, enhancing brand awareness, consolidating the company's reputation and growing a network of engaged and enthusiastic followers.

Content can be educational, informational, entertaining or promotional. Posts can be about the industry, the company or the team. Available formats include videos, images, text, documents, polls and articles.

When creating content for your Page, it is crucial to understand that you are building on three pillars with your followers – persuading them to know, like and trust your business.

Posting content will always be a balance of your resources, and the time it will take. Remember, we are aiming for consistency. Three posts per week is a good, manageable number. On the other hand, you may find that once or twice a week is all you can fit in if you are starting.

Overview of post formats

Text – the simplest form of posts on Pages is the text post. Text posts contain nothing but words, emojis, tags (@mentions), and hashtags. They are a maximum of 3,000 characters long but typically around 1,200-1,500 characters. However, they can appear plain compared with other formats, so they are less commonly seen than other types of posts, despite their potential higher view numbers.

Image + Text – a highly utilised post format because of their visual impact. Attention-grabbing images perform well and can be a graphic, photo, meme etc. However, it is vital to avoid having this format of post look visually like a paid ad. Avoid heavily branded images and make them as humanised as possible. The suggested image size is 1,080 x 1,080 pixels.

Video – an increasingly popular form of posting on LinkedIn. With most people owning smartphones and an abundance of apps that make it easy for everyone to create videos, many more people are doing so. They are best recorded in horizontal 16:9 format to display correctly in the home feed.

Talking head videos (where a person is speaking and captions underneath) are the most common and most achievable for those with a small or no budget. Videos should be short – 30-180 seconds – and always have closed captions for speech for accessibility, and also because the majority of videos are played without sound.

Document – these have the same advantages as image posts in terms of visibility in the newsfeed. In addition, they are ideal for publishing checklists, tip sheets, how-to, and slide presentations etc. The most commonly used file formats are allowed (Word, PowerPoint etc.) and are automatically turned into a PDF when published.

These posts can also be called carousel or slider posts, where a series of images have been turned into a multi-page PDF. The best size for these images is 1,080 x 1,080 pixels.

Poll – a great way to ask a question, polls are ideal for canvassing opinions, sparking debate and finding out what your audience thinks about issues. One question up to 140 characters long is allowed per poll, with 2-4 answers, each up to 30 characters. Polls can be left up for one day, three days, one week or two weeks. Only those who vote can see the results while the Poll is still open, and only Page admins can see the identity of those who have voted.

Article – long-form content has long been the missing link in the Page posting line-up but was made available in 2021. Articles posted on a Page now reside in the Articles tab under Posts. They look the same as articles from personal Profiles and have the same functionality – text formatting and embedding images, videos, slides, links, and snippets.

They can be added to the Featured section of a personal Profile by copying the URL of the article. It is expected that Google will index articles from Pages in the same way it does for Profile articles, so they are searchable. This provides an added incentive to upload Articles to Pages.

Link post – this is not an official post type but is often seen on LinkedIn. Usually made up of a hyperlink to an external site accompanied by text, this is a common way of sharing content. When a link is added to a post, LinkedIn automatically generates a preview of the site it refers to below the text. This preview image can be kept or taken out, as needed. If leaving the image in, the text containing the URL can be removed, and clicking the link will still open it.

When a full-length link is included in a post, LinkedIn automatically truncates it, so it looks like this with a green tick in front: https://lnkd.in/gDt4uA7m. However, the link does not truncate until you hit the Post button.

Whilst every post format type has advantages and disadvantages, to improve the performance of your posts, rotate through the different formats to see what resonates best with your audience.

One other factor to keep in mind, is that the LinkedIn algorithm factors in the length of time that a Page follower spends consuming the posted content. This is known as "dwell time". So the longer you can hold the attention; theoretically, your post is rewarded with further reach.

Success with publishing on LinkedIn comes from experimenting. Try different styles. Some you will enjoy creating, some may take more effort. In the same way that we all learn in different ways, we also enjoy different content styles. There is no one-size-fits-all prescription to what will work. There is only what will work for your business and your Page followers.

Suggested content plan

An excellent way to keep your Page on track is to rotate your post formats covering the following areas. Here's what this could look like for your business:

- Big Picture – industry thought leadership. Trends, innovations, concerns, regulatory changes, new laws, etc. These posts can be curated content – links to articles published elsewhere – but should be accompanied by your organisation's opinion or take on the topic.

- Human Interest – are you a purpose-led company doing work in the community? Maybe you sponsor a local team, donate to or volunteer at a particular charity. Perhaps one of your employees is presenting at an industry event. If any of these apply, take photos wherever possible and share or write about them. This both promotes the organisation you support and reflects well on your company.

- Products and Services – if you post too often about what you do or are always aiming to drive traffic to your website via links, you will scare followers away. Even when promoting your business, think in terms of what your audience wants to know about. Put yourself in their shoes and answer their questions or show how you solve their challenges. How To's and expert tips are excellent examples in this category.

Page posts lend themselves to several techniques: series, repurposing and themes.

Series – a series of posts about a particular topic is often used to break up a longer piece, perhaps an article. Several smaller posts can be created from the one Article, which is then posted individually, sometimes in succession, sometimes with other posts in between.

Once the series is published, the entire Article they were taken from can be published as long-form content, complete with additional links, images or video that may not have been included in the individual posts. Posts may or may not refer to others in the series, but the advantage of posting in this manner is that a more significant number of people can be reached and potentially drawn into the topic.

Repurposing – reusing content in different formats is a common technique that makes content creation more cost-effective. The more times the same piece of copy can be used, the more cost-effective it becomes. One of the advantages of repurposing is the larger audience that might be attracted to it, given that some people prefer to read text, some to watch a video, some to work through slides and others to consume information via images.

When written well, one piece of copy can be used as a text post (or posts), edited into a list and posted as an image, recorded and published as a video, or turned into a slide presentation for a document post.

Themes – choosing a theme for a limited time, for instance, a calendar month, allows for a variety of posts on a particular topic. It also allows it to be discussed from different angles, divided into sub-topics and published in various formats. It can include curated content or other experts' opinions, reflect what's in the news, or be treated in multiple different ways.

Rotating content fortnightly through this model will ensure you have a good variety of content and are not too focused on your company.

Repurposing existing content that you have used internally is also a suitable method.

Getting the most from posting on your Page

As with content posted from personal Profiles, posts from Pages are sent to a subset of their followers (believed to be around 3%) when they are first published. Depending on the level of response, they are then sent to a more significant number of followers. And so on.

A simple yet often overlooked strategy to encourage responses in the comments to drive the algorithm to share the post further, is to begin or end each post with a question. Inviting your audience to participate in the conversation rather than talking at them has a higher likelihood of followers commenting. Be sure to respond to every comment as quickly as practical.

To have the best chance of posts being widely seen, the Page first needs to be 100% complete. LinkedIn advises that Pages with complete information get 30% more weekly views. They also suggest that companies that post weekly see a 2x lift in engagement with their content. Consistent actions over time will ensure success.

Another technique for greater view count is to ensure the first group of followers who receive the post in their feed are targeted. This can be done through the Targeted Audience option. When inputting the post, there is an option to send it to Anyone (the default choice) or a Targeted Audience.

If you choose Targeted Audience, you are offered several filters – some useful, some less so. These filters include language, location, industry, region, job function, company size, university and seniority. Choosing one or more of these filters reduces the size of the audience who will see your post.

So, while targeting your audience to reach more relevant followers early on sounds like a good idea, it only works well if you have enough followers to make it worthwhile. Given that the target audience size needs to be at least 300, this is an excellent option for Pages with large follower numbers but not for those with a small following.

Employee support of content

The more employees you can get involved with and the faster they engage with a post, the greater the reach that post will achieve.

'Notify Employees' is a notification button you can use only once every 24 hours to prevent spamming members. LinkedIn sends the notification to those employees it believes it is most relevant to. Unfortunately, we do not know how it determines relevancy.

For such notifications to work effectively, the employees' Experience section of their Profile must be updated and linked to the Page as their current employer. It is a great idea to make this part of the onboarding process with new hires.

Setting up an internal messaging system on platforms such as email, WhatsApp, Teams, Trello, Slack etc., can also be helpful.

Having employees engage on Page posts gives you two benefits. It sparks the algorithm into sharing posts more widely and shows posts to those employees' connections. Even if you have naysayers who complain that only employees engage on Page posts, this is not a reason to stop.

Posting quality posts consistently will, over time, see your posts attract engagement from others. Think of it as the dance floor at a wedding. No one wants to be first up, but others more readily follow once the first person does.

Having incentives in place for supportive employees will go a long way. It is often overlooked and an unspoken expectation. A supportive employee of social content is worth their weight in gold so recognise this effort.

Pinning a post

LinkedIn offers the option of pinning one post to the top of the Page feed. This is an ideal place to welcome visitors to the Page and encourage them to follow and explain the content they will find. If this option is not enabled, posts are generally displayed chronologically, with the most recent first.

Posting mistakes to avoid

Before beginning to post on your Page, it is essential to know what NOT to do. You are acting as a representative of your organisation, whether you are the owner or the social media manager, so it is imperative to follow accepted best practices – not only those for general writing but also those particular to LinkedIn.

1. Do not start posting until you have a top-notch Page. This means having all the components listed in Chapter 4 complete and up to date. Most important is easily accessible contact details.

2. Do not publish one big block of text without line breaks. It will be unreadable and discourage people from reading your post. Instead, break up blocks of text into one to two sentence paragraphs and add a blank line between them. The exception to this is using a bulleted list with emojis. If these are short, they look better when placed on immediately consecutive lines.

3. Do not tag half a dozen irrelevant people in the post, hoping they will comment. This does not work and can be detrimental to your post if they do not respond. A better course of action is to tag them in a comment below the post or use the Send button to direct message the post to them. If you tag a person, it will show up in their notifications, but they need to be looking there. A DM (direct message) is more likely to be seen as unread messages are bold in the message feed and sit at the bottom of the screen in blue.

4. The current best practice for hashtags is 3-5 per post. There is no indication that more add value. Hashtags look better displayed as a list at the end of the post, but they can also sit on one line. It is not

best practice to turn some of the keywords in your post into hashtags as this reduces readability.

What you focus on in your hashtags will depend on your company, but options are:

- The three listed in your Page's Overview section (see image)

- One unique that relates to your industry and summarises your topic (e.g. #CompanyName #Retail #CustomerLoyalty)

- Hashtags that have the highest number of followers (e.g. #DigitalMarketing has 27.5 million followers).

LinkedIn is expected to use hashtags in a more overt, powerful way in future. If this is the case, it follows that setting up a unique hashtag relevant only to your company will help attract Page followers. Your company name as a hashtag is the most common way to do this.

5. Do not use the same content from other social media platforms and publish it on LinkedIn without tailoring it for the LinkedIn audience and platform. It isn't a problem to repurpose content, but each platform has nuances you must always be mindful of.

6. Do not constantly publish promotional posts that are all about the company. Instead, share information of value if you expect people to give up their time to read it. We come to LinkedIn in part to learn from others, so make sure your company is seen as the expert in its field by providing high-quality informational and educational material that helps clients in their work. By always promoting the company or trying to sell your products or services, you will lose credibility when the aim is to build it.

7. Check the text for errors before publishing. This applies to the text accompanying the post and the content itself if it's a document, video or image. Nothing makes a company look sloppy and unprofessional more than poorly worded or error-ridden text.

Post frequency

Aim for three times a week if resources allow. However, posting twice a week consistently is better than three posts one week, zero the next, five after that, and then one etc. If two posts per week are what you can sustain over the long haul, stick with two, but do so every week without exception.

Your Page will perform much more strongly if you show up week after week than if you publish lots of posts for only a month. Publishing regularly is about developing trust as a company. We all build trust with our personal Profiles, but Page posts are about building the company's reputation as trustworthy, credible, knowledgeable, consistent, professional and helpful.

Do not expect to receive high organic reach when you begin posting suddenly. It takes time to build up. But if you post consistently and gradually build your follower numbers, the views will come.

Another caveat with posts to note is that some posts will do better than others. It can be tough to determine the high performers as the algorithm is full of unknowns. However, publishing quality content regularly while building followers will inevitably result in greater organic reach.

Post metrics

LinkedIn provides a few key metrics on posts. These include impressions, reactions, click-through rate, comments, shares, clicks and engagement rate.

Engagement rate is calculated as:

$$\frac{(Likes + Comments + Shares + Clicks + Follows)}{Impressions}$$

It is worth noting that views or impressions do not indicate the number of people who have seen or read your post. That number is merely the number of newsfeeds into which LinkedIn has placed your post. A better gauge of the success of a post is engagement rate and is a metric to aim at improving over time.

One way to encourage engagement is to use the Notify employees button to alert them when a new post has been published. However, this is a hit-and-miss strategy as it relies on them seeing the notifications. It is much better to have dedicated posting days and times, so employees can check themselves without being reminded.

In the newsfeed and when visiting a Page, the first few lines of each post are displayed. After that, up to five lines are visible depending on how a person views the post and whether there is only text or text and another component such as an image or video. This makes those first few lines the most important in 'stopping the scroll'.

When the algorithm senses the viewer has stopped to read the post or clicks See more, it concludes the post is of interest to that person. It then does two things: places more posts of similar content into the viewer's newsfeed and places the post into other newsfeeds to extend its reach.

Gold Nuggets

- Publishing content from your Page will enhance brand awareness, build a strong network and give you credibility and visibility.

- Quality posts published less frequently is a better strategy than poor posts published more often.

- Using all the different post formats available will attract a wider audience than using just one.

- Plan your content to cover the big picture, human interest and product/services.

- Encourage your key team members to engage on the company's posts to increase view numbers. Have the leadership team lead by example.

Chapter 6
How to Grow LinkedIn Pages

Gaining a solid network of followers for your Page is not difficult, but it will take time. The biggest mistake you can make is to give up too early. If your business is starting from scratch, allow an absolute minimum of six months to start to see traction. Remember, a Page with a strong community of followers is a long-term asset.

Should you go for quality or quantity? For example, should you invite people you know are potential customers or clients only, or do you invite all your connections to follow your Page?

There is never a one-size-fits-all prescription for success. Instead, the answer will depend on a wide range of factors such as, but not limited, to:

- Business – the number of employees, the resources available such as people and budget, the ideal client Profile, the age of the business etc

- Business goals – brand awareness, lead generation, overall social media strategy etc

- Personal LinkedIn strategy – activity levels, connections, content frequency, confidence, focus etc.

What also comes into play is the LinkedIn algorithm. Whilst we never really know exactly how it works, we can share our knowledge from our extensive personal experience and research of current best practices on LinkedIn.

At the time of writing, it is estimated that Page posts are placed in only a tiny percentage of Page followers' feeds (estimated to be approximately 3% versus 10% for personal posts).

Here are some suggested strategies for consideration based on your knowledge of your business and goals.

Strategy 1 – Brand Awareness

If your strategy is brand awareness, you would be inclined to invite a wide spectrum of your followers (for instance, all connections whose names begin with J in one month). Again, this is highly suited to companies that offer more generic services that have a broad audience.

Strategy 2 – Niche Community

If your business targets a particular niche in the market, your strategy to grow the Page followers should match this. This could be targeted by geography, industry, job position etc. It may take longer to grow Page followers using a niche strategy, but it will be a highly concentrated pool of followers and offer a much higher chance of lead generation.

Strategy 3 – Account-Based Marketing

If your strategy targets particular businesses and develops customer relationships, your invite strategy would best be targeted and niche. The invitation credit filters would be an excellent tool to ensure you invite by your current company.

Being clear on your objective before you begin will ensure you choose the right strategy for your business. After all, there is no point in inviting anyone and everyone you are connected to if your Page will simply be of no interest to them. That would be counterproductive to your reputation.

No matter which strategy you choose, it is critical to make sure the Page content matches the strategy and focus to fast track your success.

How you use LinkedIn is also a determinant of Page follower growth. While most of your growth will likely come from inviting people, a certain percentage of people will follow you when they see posts in their newsfeed that they like. If your topic resonates with them, they will follow you without being asked so they can read more of your material and not miss out on anything important to them. If you do not post quality content, they are less likely to come across your Page and feel inclined to follow it.

But, for most of us, growing a targeted Page following quickly is our initial aim. If your LinkedIn resources are limited, you'll be pleased to know that growing your follower numbers is not as arduous a task as you might think. Just a few minutes a day will see your network grow steadily.

LinkedIn allows you to send 100 invites to connections each month. For every person who accepts and becomes a Page follower, LinkedIn gives you that invite back as a credit to invite another person. If your invites are well-targeted – for instance, new connections or industry connections – it will take approximately six to eight months to reach the magic 500 followers.

As mentioned elsewhere in this book, a Page following of between 500 and 1,000 is where the magic begins. Posts start to gain traction with that base as you have built a critical mass of followers who will be familiar with your content. As you refine what works, you will only get a better response.

However, what do you do if your personal connection numbers are low and you run out of people to invite? First, you should continually be growing your personal network. In her book *Link-Ability, 4 powerful strategies to maximise your LinkedIn success*, co-author of this book Lynnaire Johnston shares her techniques for building an extensive network of valuable connections.

But if it is more important to you to have a greater following on your Page than on your Profile, there is another option. Additional team members can be given Super Admin access, and this will allow them to send out invitations to their connections. Having the executive team included in this process is essential, as is the sales team.

Rotate this role around your team members, and if everyone is active on LinkedIn, there should always be new people to invite. LinkedIn may eventually relax the rules around inviting only connections to follow Pages, but currently, this is not the case.

Another source of new Page followers is your team. Ideally, you will be listed as their employer on their personal Profile in the Experience section, automatically making them a Page follower. Keep in mind that the quality of their personal Profile reflects on you, the company. Organisations, where all the listed employees (publicly viewable by anyone) have high-quality Profiles, send an exceedingly positive message to potential customers or clients.

The best time to ask someone to follow your Page is when they first connect with you personally. If you have sent them a personalised invite (when you're inviting them) and have responded to their acceptance with a personalised follow-up message, that's the time to send a Page invite. The same is true if they have invited you to connect.

Follow up immediately on your 'thank you for connecting' message with a Page invite. This is especially true if you are well known, have name recognition or are an expert in your field, and they have connected with you to gain the benefit of your knowledge.

The Invite Connections to Follow section sits on the right of your Page's Home Page. If it is not visible, you can access it from the Admin tools drop-down menu. It provides a list of people you might want to invite but don't feel you need to follow this. It's easy to type in the first few letters of the name of the connections you do want to invite, and the autofill will do the rest. It also tells you how many invites you have left for the month. It returns to 100 at the start of each month, whether or not you have used all the previous month's allocation. If you don't use them, you lose them.

An excellent method of gaining followers organically – without having to invite them individually – is to add a 'follow our Page' line at the end of each personal post beside your hashtags.

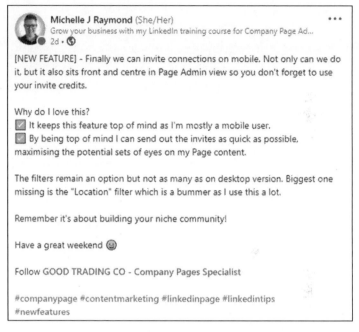

Gaining followers organically through posts is another good reason to regularly and frequently publish value-added material that people want to read. (Read more about this in chapter 5).

It's also possible to set up a personalised company hashtag, e.g. #GoodTradingCo

Share the Page as a post or direct message

LinkedIn provides two other ways to encourage people to become Page followers – Share in a post and Send in a message. These options sit under the Share Page tab directly underneath the Page banner, at the right.

When you choose the Share Page in a post, LinkedIn provides default post text which reads: *'Want to stay up-to-date with what is going on? Follow our Page for the latest updates.'* Below is a link to the Page which people click to visit the Page and hopefully follow it. We strongly advise against using this message and tactic without giving potential followers an excellent reason to go to the Page. Otherwise, it seems entirely self-serving and does nothing to build a relationship between the Page and the follower.

When you choose to Share a Page as a message, the default text is: *'Want to stay up-to-date with what is going on? Follow our Page for the latest updates.'* In our opinion, this is not the type of message that would resonate well with business professionals, so write one that is more in line with your company messaging and is more personal to the invitee.

However you decide to grow your Page following – through invites, sharing via post or DM – increasing your network size will be vital to your ongoing success with Pages. Without this, your posts will be seen by fewer people, and your visibility will be hampered. Including Page follower growth as a key strategy will work significantly in your organisations' favour.

Eight Ways to Increase Page Followers

1. Utilise your invite credits each month

2. Use the Share Page button to invite people to follow the Page

3. Use a hyperlink to your Page in email signatures

4. Install the LinkedIn Follow Company plugin button [https://bit.ly/3mMANtc] on your website

5. Ensure all staff have their LinkedIn Profile work experience updated

6. Highlight Page following as part of employee onboarding

7. Organic growth comes from good-quality content that adds value. Share your company expertise

8. If you have a premium LinkedIn account, try using the out-of-office messaging service as a creative way to highlight your Page

Gold Nuggets

- Grow the size of your Page followers consistently through organic reach and personal invitation.

- Invite only those people to whom your Page will be relevant.

- Encourage your staff or team members to follow your Page by adding you as their employer on their personal Profiles.

- Post quality content regularly to help organic Page growth.

- Don't give up! This will take time, just like growing your business. However, the hard part is the beginning, and over time you will gain momentum.

Chapter 7
How to Set up and Run Events on Pages

When using the LinkedIn platform to grow your reach and engagement, an excellent tool is the Events feature. This is a great way to leverage the community of followers you have also been actively building on your Page on a trusted platform.

LinkedIn is constantly refining the functionality of Events, allowing them to be promoted more widely and therefore attract more attendees.

Events are supported by LinkedIn, which helps with organic discovery. Here are some of the ways they do this:

- Upcoming events can be discovered through the Events tab on your Page

- The My Network tab on Profiles contains personalised event recommendations

- Events are easily shared in a post, and LinkedIn notifies a relevant subset of your followers

- Your event stands out with a highly visual banner and a prominent CTA button when shared to the feed.

There are also paid strategy options available to amplify and extend your target reach.

There are two main types of events:

1. Events held off LinkedIn – for example, face-to-face, Zoom, which may or may not require registration to attend

2. LinkedIn Lives – events held in real-time on the LinkedIn platform.

To hold a LinkedIn Live, you need to apply for and be granted access to broadcast by LinkedIn. You also need a third-party streaming service such as StreamYard, Restream, Social Live etc.

Approval for Live Access for Pages is granted quickly if you meet the criteria, such as a minimum of 150 Page followers. (Details of the criteria can be found at https://business.linkedin.com/marketing-solutions/linkedin-live).

It is also possible to use your Page to publicise events on other platforms such as Zoom and Facebook Live, and this is an excellent way to increase attendance at your event.

The benefits of holding events via Pages

Events are an easy way to connect with your existing Page followers and attract potential new followers. They are easy to set up, invite connections, and have considerable functionality, including chat, posting, analytics, and a unique URL.

You have the option to choose between a registered event or a non-registered one. Both have pros and cons and again should tie back to your goals of brand awareness or lead generation.

For registered events, Super Admins and Content Admins of a Page can collect data from events they're hosting by using pre-filled registration forms with LinkedIn Profile data. Users opt-in or out of future marketing and promotion follow up. This helps those who are looking to build email lists for future marketing initiatives.

Whilst the temptation is to run an event merely to expand your email list, we recommend caution. Any follow-up from the event should be valuable and avoid appearing to be spam. Registered events can also have less reach and engagement as they are not promoted in the feed by LinkedIn.

The most significant advantage of hosting an event on LinkedIn is building person-to-person relationships with Page followers. In addition, you will have a list of attendees whom you can message and connect with. So, before you consider people as 'leads', think of them as people.

Our experience is that creating an Event on LinkedIn is an excellent way to market it. While it can be time-consuming to send invites, the response generated more than makes up for this. Also, it doesn't matter whether the Page has 400 or 4,000 followers; the invitation list comes from the connections of the Super and Content admins.

How to set up an event

Under Admin tools on the Page, click Create event. You will be prompted for a title, description, event details (venue, date and time etc.), and the registration link. Once completed, the event is given its unique Page with a URL. From here, you can invite connections, see who's attending, look at analytics, operate a chat section, create a poll and upload posts. Finally, the Manage event tab allows you to edit the event, manage attendees and cancel the event.

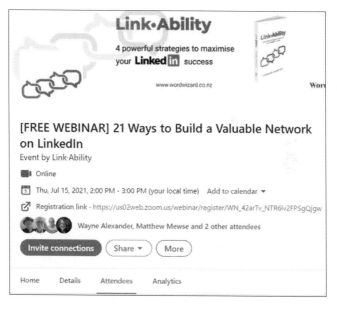

Once your event is set up, you can begin to invite connections. Those who accept will be offered the opportunity to invite connections, too. The ripple out effect of this could be significant. For example, if 10 staff members accept the invitation to attend and invite 10 connections (preferably more), the number who can be reached could be considerably larger than just connections from the main Page admin alone. The limit on the number of connections that can be invited is 1,000 per admin per week. This is a total limit across all Events for that week.

The invitations sent by LinkedIn do not include many details of the Event, and the temptation for recipients is to accept the invitation when they receive it and not look further. This can be an issue when the event is held off-platform such as on Zoom and requires a separate registration.

Many people assume that by accepting the invite, they will automatically have access to the event.

Unfortunately, while the Event Page shows the registration link in the details at the top, many people appear to miss this.

There are several ways to solve this problem.

- Host the event and registration within LinkedIn. This is the simplest and most highly recommended way to avoid any confusion.

- Frequently add the link in the chat with a reminder about registering.

- Use the event feed to post about the event and a registration reminder. Make it the top post in the feed so that those trying to join late can easily find the link.

- Message those who accept the invite with more details. This is, however, time-consuming if the numbers accepting are large.

LinkedIn will continue to improve the Events space with extension into paid events expected soon. Where possible, always try to host and promote the Event within LinkedIn.

When someone accepts an invitation to an event, it is added to the Events tab on their Manage my Network Page and their Home Page. In addition, visitors to their Profile will see it in their Highlights section. They are also sent an email which says: '[Name], you're attending [FREE WEBINAR] 21 Ways to Build a Valuable Network on LinkedIn' with an option for adding it to their calendar.

Highlights

1 Mutual Group
You and Matthew are both in Growing Dunedin's Economy

[FREE WEBINAR] 21 Ways to Build a Valuable Network on LinkedIn
Matthew is attending this event

(Message)

People who accept the invitation can also post on the Event Page. This is a good place to ask people to drop their questions before the event so the speakers can prepare suitable answers.

When you visit LinkedIn Pages as a member, an Events tab highlights both upcoming and past events. As an Admin, find your planned events by going to the Manage section on the right of the Page Admin home view.

When a person who is attending uploads a post about the event from the Event Page, it appears in their normal newsfeed, giving plenty of opportunity for reaction and comment.

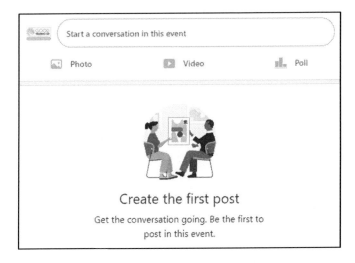

Start a conversation in this event

Photo   Video   Poll

Create the first post
Get the conversation going. Be the first to post in this event.

Post-event activities

When a public event is over, the Event Page remains live. Here you can add the replay link or any other details you want attendees to know about. The attendees' list also remains. Access to this is via the Page URL or the Event section on the right of the Page. Previous events are listed under a tab labelled Past.

If you have created a registered Event, you can download a .csv file of the attendees.

An additional advantage of creating Events on LinkedIn is that your event will continue to show up in the Highlights section of attendees even after the event is over. It displays the Page logo, event name, and that [name] attended this event. This is a great promotion for your business and event, especially if you hold it regularly.

Highlights

4 Mutual Groups
You and Wayne are both in New Zealand SME Business Network, Growing Dunedin's Economy, and 2 others

[FREE WEBINAR] 21 Ways to Build a Valuable Network on LinkedIn
Wayne attended this event

(Message)

Gold Nuggets

- Organising and managing an event on LinkedIn is an excellent way to extend the company's reach and is a popular lead generation tool.

- LinkedIn has combined Live and Events for Pages to give users the best features of each type of Event.

- Posts, analytics and other functions allow interaction between event attendees and the organisers.

- If the event requires external registration, it is wise to let attendees know this and re-share the link. Where possible, try to run the whole Event through LinkedIn tools to avoid confusion.

Chapter 8
LinkedIn Page Sub-Pages and How to Use Them

LinkedIn offers several additional sub-Pages that supplement the main LinkedIn Page. Collectively, these are known as Affiliate Pages and can include Showcase Pages, Product Pages, plus Acquisition and Subsidiary Pages.

As no two businesses are the same, again, we reiterate there is no one-size-fits-all prescription. But before you rush in to set up one of these sub-Pages, consider the following:

- The size of your company
- How many companies does your business own
- The number of divisions or brands
- The internal resources available for managing the Page/s
- The goals of the business.

A company's related sub-Pages are grouped in the right column of its Home Page under the title Affiliated Pages. The exception is Product Pages which have their own tab on the Page's Home navigation bar.

The image below shows the Affiliated Pages on Adobe's Page, which are listed as Showcase Page, Subsidiary and Acquisition.

When the See all Affiliated Pages tab is selected, the entire range of these sub-Pages displays as below. For example, you can see Adobe has three Showcase Pages, two Acquisition Pages and two Subsidiary Pages.

Let's look at each of these types of Pages.

Showcase Page

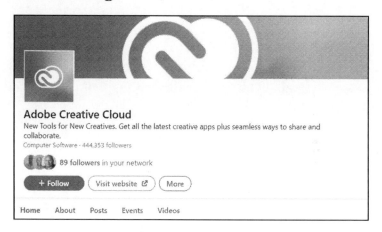

A Showcase Page allows companies to separate their product lines or services into separate Pages on which they detail their offering. For example, if you are a large accounting firm, you might have a Showcase Page for each business area, e.g. taxation, business, property etc. A legal firm might have Showcase Pages for family law, commercial, conveyancing, criminal etc. The Adobe Showcase Page (above) shares information about new tools for creatives.

To reach a Page's Showcase Page, tap or click on the Showcase Page name. To follow the Page, click one of the Follow buttons on the Page.

LinkedIn describes Showcase Pages as dedicated to representing a brand, business unit, or organisation's initiative, and not for short-term marketing campaigns.

How to set up a Showcase Page

You must be a Super Admin of the Page to create a Showcase Page. Up to 25 Showcase Pages can be created for each Page.

From the Admin tools menu, click Create a Showcase Page.

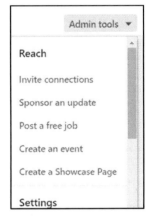

Complete the details in the fields displayed.

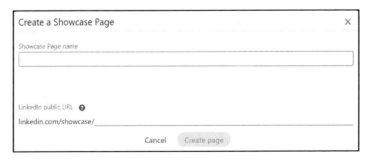

Once your Showcase Page is set up, it will display under Affiliated Pages in the right column on the Page's Home Page.

The complete Page looks like this:

Inviting people to follow the Showcase Page works the same as for a Page. Each month, 100 people can be invited to follow the Showcase Page, with acceptances returning a credit for another invite to be sent.

Posts published on a Showcase Page will/may appear in the feeds of its followers.

Before considering using a Showcase Page, consider your resourcing. If you are a small to medium business with limited resources, this may not be the right strategy as it is essentially a duplication of effort.

Also, a limitation of Showcase Pages is that they do not have employees, and therefore, you can't notify employes that content has been posted.

Product Pages

A Page can have up to 35 related Product Pages on which to showcase the organisation's products. Product Pages display on the Page's Home Page under a tab labelled Product. Currently, LinkedIn must approve product Pages before they are displayed on your Page.

Until recently, Product Pages were only available for companies offering digital products, e.g. software, SAAS etc. However, they are now slowly rolling out to other market segments, which is great news for Page owners because they have unique and useful features.

A Product Page allows you to build up social proof using:

- Featured customers
- Product videos and screenshots
- Recommendations
- Community hashtags
- Adding skills to personal Profiles.

Companies can highlight major customers who use the product, displayed in the Featured customers' section.

Page admins can invite users to write Recommendations that are visible to visitors of the Product Page. This is done using the 'Copy request link', which can be sent via email or direct message. Page admins can then choose whether recommendations are visible or hidden.

LinkedIn users can also easily add the product as a skill on their Profile quickly and easily with the click of a button.

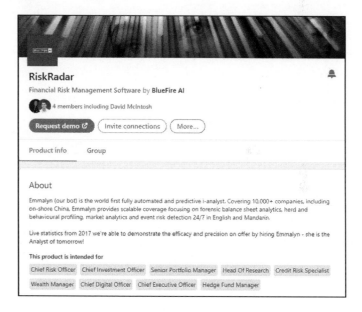

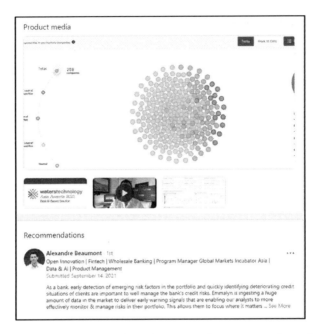

If your company qualifies for a Product Page, here's how to create it:

- In Super or Content admin, click the Products tab in the top navigation. (If you cannot see this, your company is not eligible for a Product Page.)

- Click the Add product button. Enter your product name and click Save. You'll be routed to your new Product Page.

- On the Product Page, enter all the required information by clicking the Edit icon next to each field and enter any additional information. Click the Add category field to see the options. If your product is a suite, you can choose more than one category. Your default hashtag will be your #productname. Custom hashtags are not currently available.

- Click the Save button for each item edited.

- Click the Submit for review button, which sends the Product Page to LinkedIn to approve. This may take up to two weeks, and you'll receive a notification in your Activity Tab once the process is complete.

Once your Product Page is created and approved, you'll need to publish it. Do this by:

- Clicking the Activity tab in the top navigation bar

- Click the View product button, then Publish product.

In addition, Groups related to Product Pages are being rolled out. This allows your community to engage in conversation and talk about your product.

Deciding if you need Company Page sub-Pages

With any of these sub-Pages, it is a juggling act between getting the right content in front of the right audience while managing the workload that comes with it. Start simple to maintain the momentum over the longer term. This will benefit you more than going hard then giving up.

If you are a small business with limited resources, it is best to keep everything under the main Page. It will be easier to manage, and you can always add in more later.

If you are a large business with multiple divisions and brands and the resources to manage them, we recommend setting up additional Showcase Pages for each brand. Keep in mind that Showcase Pages are used to highlight your unique brands, business units or initiatives. As well, they allow you to have targeted content for each niche.

For example, ACME Co has multiple unrelated divisions, e.g. Food, Cleaning Products, Beauty, Industrial etc. A Showcase Page for each division allows ACME to make the content relevant to each audience. This provides a higher chance of engagement.

Every Showcase Page you create will need relevant content created and published on a consistently regular basis. It will also need an audience of followers. This takes effort and resources that you may not have internally.

If you have limited resources, then we recommend you hold off on Showcase Pages. You are best suited to manage the multiple divisions by rotating content frequently to highlight the different components of your business.

Subsidiary and Acquisition Pages

Affiliate Pages are used when an organisation wants its affiliations or initiatives to be more visible to its followers. For example, suppose one company is acquired by another but remains a separate working entity and its products continue to function under the existing brand. In that case, it might have an Affiliate Page on the acquiring company's Page, labelled either Subsidiary or Acquisition, as in the Adobe example earlier in this chapter. To set up either of these Affiliate Pages, a request must be made to LinkedIn.

Acquisition and Subsidiary Pages are designed for large and enterprise-sized organisations and are not generally suitable for small companies.

Gold Nuggets

- The Experience section of personal Profiles cannot be linked to Showcase Pages.

- Affiliated Pages are either a Showcase, Product, Subsidiary or Acquisition Page.

- Each sub-Page has a different purpose, audience and set-up requirement and needs resources to be managed effectively.

- Small businesses with limited resources are advised not to venture into sub-Pages.

Part 3 — Advantage

Chapter 9
Gold Standard LinkedIn Pages Worth Following

This chapter highlights examples of the many LinkedIn Page concepts we have already discussed so you can see them in action.

Just as no two companies are alike, no two Pages are the same. The Pages we share come from various industries, are a range of sizes and highlight best practices for Pages. Looking at Pages from industries other than your own can spark ideas that will help ensure your Page stands out from others.

Don't fall into the trap of trying to copy or emulate another Page because it is successful. Successful Pages are more than just clever copy. They are a reflection of their employees, brand values, leadership and policies. Make your Page unique to your organisation.

A Page with a large following does not necessarily represent best practice. Large workforces can influence this and often mirror how their Page is set up and managed on other platforms.

We suggest you review the examples shared here on a case-by-case basis to see what they are doing well and how this might apply to your business.

Take the gold from each and use that to power your Page. Choose what works best to highlight your unique selling proposition.

Shield –
https://www.linkedin.com/company/shieldapp/

Shield is a great example of using content to help promote employees who are heavily focused on building their personal brands. Building up your employees as a go-to authority is as important as building employee advocacy for the company.

The content formats they use are rotated, and their posts are always helpful. They speak to the audience's pain points – LinkedIn users wanting to get the most out of their time on LinkedIn.

Gong IO –
https://www.linkedin.com/company/gong-io/

Gong has a unique, fun content style that is heavily text-based and instantly recognisable. The format of text posts is consistent, relatively short and directed at audiences looking to build revenue.

Besides attracting potential new clients, Gong's Page is also used to attract top talent. The photos give you an instant feel for what it would be like to work at Gong.

Good Trading Co –
https://www.linkedin.com/company/good-trading-co-linkedin4business

This is the Page of co-author Michelle J Raymond and educates Page admins, business owners and agencies to get the most out of Pages to boost their reputation and revenue.

Michelle sits on the Small Business Advisory Council to the Product team responsible for LinkedIn Pages. New features are always rolled out first to this Page and shared with the community, making this a very good Page to follow to keep abreast of changes and updates.

The Good Trading Co Page highlights strategies, features and content styles that you too can use in your LinkedIn marketing.

Netflix –
https://www.linkedin.com/company/netflix/

This instantly recognisable global brand with approximately 7.5 million followers is one of the largest Pages highlighted here. However, it's not the enormous follower count that's important but the great way the Page demonstrates its values through its content.

They tie these values back to the shows they are releasing but at no time do you feel like this is an advert.

The Page also heavily promotes sustainability, diversity, equity and inclusivity themes which can be seen in the powerful use of the banner space.

Dandi Day – Conscious Beauty Community –
https://www.linkedin.com/company/dandi-day

Simon Sinek says, 'Start with Your Why,' which is exactly what the Dandi Day Page does. It's an outstanding example of using a Page to build a niche community of like-minded people within an industry. In this case, the niche is sustainable beauty.

The Page content is used to educate their community of followers on sustainability and share expert tips on making sustainable choices. This also creates a platform to cross-promote collaborative partners with related services that help sustainable beauty businesses following the Page.

Semrush –
https://www.linkedin.com/company/semrush/

Semrush is a leading online visibility management SaaS platform used by 7 million digital marketers worldwide. The content is both practical and easy to consume.

Multiple Product Pages highlight the various digital products they offer. Each Product Page details the intended product and product media, such as videos and featured customers. The customised button Trial Now is an excellent tool for lead generation as it redirects to a specific landing Page.

They are extremely active in responding when the Page is tagged with comments.

The Semrush Products Page can be seen at:
https://www.linkedin.com/products/semrush-trends/

Chorus NZ –
https://www.linkedin.com/company/chorus-nz-limited/

Chorus NZ is New Zealand's largest telecommunications utility, rolling out ultra-fast broadband (UFB) to 75% of the country's fibre customers.

The content on this Page could easily just focus on technology updates. But, instead, it moves beyond this, to the impact on the local community and how it makes life easier.

Showing the human side of the business and focus on community, the content answers the question – how can technology be used for better living? They answer popular questions that potential customers ask and rotate content formats to keep the Page interesting.

Franchise-Info –
https://www.linkedin.com/company/franchise-info-sponsored/

'Welcome to the Franchising News Hub on LinkedIn.' This text comes from the About section on this Page of carefully curated content on the franchise industry, perfectly summing up why it is successful.

The team set out to build a community around a niche and put in consistent effort to develop a significant audience to circulate a newsletter and generate other business opportunities.

This Page is a great example of what can be built with consistent effort over time.

How to find examples of Pages relevant to your industry

A simple method is to use keywords in the search function and go to the Company filter tab. This will list related Pages and the number of followers of each Page.

Looking to other Pages for inspiration is always sensible. Still, it doesn't replace Page administrators' analysis with learning what content works best for their unique follower base. In addition, there can be differences between industries, geographies and target markets that must always be factored in.

Pages are never static – new ones arrive, older ones disappear. Many are set up and forgotten. Some are created to provide a logo for a personal Profile. But if you are a Page admin or a business owner, looking at ways to use your Page in your marketing will pay dividends.

Chapter 10
The Future of LinkedIn Pages

To predict the future of LinkedIn Pages, one might think it requires a highly polished crystal ball. Unfortunately, LinkedIn is not generally forthcoming with its strategy or plans for the platform. So typically, as new features are rolled out, the collective users surmise what it could all mean in the big scheme of things.

However, we know that LinkedIn highly values their status as a most trusted platform, always guiding its decision-making. Some may say they are slow to adapt and add new features, but the platform has stood the test of time.

As with every social media platform, LinkedIn will continue to evolve and look for new ways to serve its nearly 800 million users best. This is why it has lasted almost 20 years with very little, if any, direct competition in the B2B and professional community space.

Rollout and expansion of Product Tab + Group

Making the Product Page function available to more than just software providers, opens many doors for companies.

There is a greater opportunity to showcase what is on offer and how it benefits customers, but peers can reach out to and talk about their experience with the company. Over time, these customer recommendations will become important social proof.

Groups historically have not delivered the results that marketers had hoped. With the addition of Groups linked to Product Pages, it will be easier to encourage your community to become evangelists for your products. LinkedIn is aware of Groups' shortcomings, and the Pages team is working behind the scenes on improvements.

Pages Articles

Whilst this functionality was only recently released, long-form articles will play a big part in the future of Pages. This might seem counterintuitive when attention spans seem to be getting shorter, but when LinkedIn released the *2021 Edelman LinkedIn B2B Thought Leadership Impact Study* [https://bit.ly/3oQpDGI], one of the key findings was that 'Quantity Rises, Whilst Quality Declines.'

The majority of decision-makers said that less than half the thought leadership they consume gives them valuable insights. So there is a real opportunity for businesses to invest in creating B2B thought leadership content that is of high value. Most of all, it should be interesting and not stuffy or overly technical. Remember, Pages need to be entertaining, not just educational.

Page Articles have the functionality to deliver this, thereby influencing decision-makers who are researching purchasing decisions online.

Pages Newsletters

Newsletters are one of the areas that the Pages development team have highlighted. This aligns with the value of companies driving industry conversations and adding value. It will be another way to leverage a niche community of followers should they become widely available.

LinkedIn Live Events

Being able to target quality over quantity is the advantage that Pages deliver to B2B marketers. As a result, we have seen many changes to the Live streaming process that enhances the integration of external platforms into LinkedIn.

LinkedIn says, 'LinkedIn Live allows you to build deeper connections and drive more engagement with the world's largest professional community. Live videos get on average 7x more reactions and 24x more comments than native video produced by the same broadcasters.

Significant changes to existing processes are being rolled out through Q4 2021. In addition, at the time of writing, there were very strong rumours that new functionality would be released that allows marketers to hold paid Live Events through the platform. This will be a game-changer and remove some current frustrations.

Having more options to make the most of a targeted community will, we believe, be extremely popular. In addition, LinkedIn has gone a step further by introducing paid advertising uniquely for Events to support this further.

Whilst it's easy to get caught up in the features of Pages, the real future is in companies leading the way to build communities and lead conversations. The functionality will support this and gives Pages an exciting future.

Influences on the future of Pages

One cannot predict the future of LinkedIn Pages without considering the seismic shift in working patterns due to COVID-19. There are two megatrends that LinkedIn sees itself as a solution provider for – the #GreatReshuffle (employees rethinking not only how they work, but why they work) and #HybridParadox (working from home gets tasks done but hampers innovation) – as the global workforce adapts. This also includes connecting companies to their target audience.

The impact of COVID-19 has made many businesses reconsider how they sell, market and transact. With the shift away from face-to-face interactions and movement towards online transactions, we will see LinkedIn follow suit.

Alongside this, companies will realise the benefits of making better use of what is essentially a free marketing platform that enables them to reach their intended audience. There are now many opportunities for businesses to promote their brand, share their product and service information, and build relationships with potential customers organically.

Many will see building communities as the way to do this through their teams or staff members, outreach via posts, events, and other activities on LinkedIn. In addition, the opportunities to involve their teams in employee advocacy and their clients as brand ambassadors are increasing. All these help companies to increase visibility, credibility and their know, like and trust factor.

The second major factor in predicting the future of Pages is that LinkedIn advertising revenue is at record levels. As you cannot run a paid ad strategy without a Page, it makes sense to make Pages more attractive. The more companies that create a Page, the higher the chance of enticing them to spend their advertising budget on the platform.

In an article published on his Profile , LinkedIn COO Daniel Shapero says, "Our customers turn to LinkedIn Marketing Services (LMS) to drive awareness and website traffic, build community, and generate leads, with 58 million companies having a Page on the platform. LMS surpassed $1 billion in quarterly revenue for the first time in Q4, up 97 per cent year over year, and the business continues to grow three times faster than the B2B digital advertising market". [https://bit.ly/3BusvMY]

The authors believe that LinkedIn will continue to make positive changes to Pages. We expect to see additional functionality rolled out to allow companies improved options to display their products and services.

LinkedIn's mantra is "do business where business is done". Their intention is clear and signals a move away from the LinkedIn of previous years that was heavily focused on HR solutions and recruitment.

For Pages, this is multifaceted, fostering buyer/seller, employer/employee, and peer/peer relationships.

Pages serve many masters – from the HR team using the Page to attract top talent to the marketing team generating leads and the sales team for social selling. Over time, and with the arrival of more functions and features, Pages' role will become increasingly integral to every company's sales and marketing strategy.

The social selling techniques used in business today are very different from the way sales were once conducted. Instead of push, push, push, the focus is on attracting opportunities. It is about creating shareable content that encourages engagements, not just followers. Using the audience to guide your activities, especially on your Page, will pay dividends, especially if your competition is not reaching customers this way.

Another aspect of selling that is still in its infancy for many smaller organisations is the understanding of the power in the team. LinkedIn understands this concept and encourages employee engagement and a sense of pride in what the organisation and colleagues are achieving through the My Company Tab.

Training and encouraging employees to become involved in the company's Page may give team members a sense of fulfilment they might not otherwise receive in the office environment. In addition, this centralised space for employees to stay connected and up to date with what is happening in the company will deliver additional benefits as time goes on.

Final Words

LinkedIn has their focus very firmly on the future. They will continue to consolidate their seemingly unassailable position as the online business tool of choice for businesses and individuals in the B2B market space by developing new features and functions.

They will continue to encourage businesses to see LinkedIn as much greater than the sum of its parts by making it easier for businesses to reach targeted audiences for a relatively low cost.

And they will continue to adapt to changing ways of working and respond to evolving trends in the world at large.

We, the authors, see only good times ahead for LinkedIn Pages and invite you to take a close look at them for your business. If you have looked in the past and were put off due to a lack of functionality, we encourage you to take a fresh look. Armed with a raft of new features and the information gleaned from this book, Pages will shine in a new light and become **Business Gold** for your organisation.

Connect with the authors on LinkedIn

Lynnaire Johnston
Compelling LinkedIn profiles
LinkedIn marketing, training, c...

Michelle J Raymond
Global LinkedIn Pages Specialist and Trainer.
Let's Connect.

Printed in Great Britain
by Amazon